8/99

The Conflict Resolution Library™

Dealing with Discrimination

• Don Middleton •

The Rosen Publishing Group's

PowerKids Press™

New York

This book is dedicated to my wife, Sue; my daughters, Jody and Kim; my mother-in-law, Mim; and my parents, Bernice and Helmut Bischoff. Also, special thanks to authors and friends Diana Star Helmer and Tom Owens for believing in me. —Don Middleton

Published in 1999 by The Rosen Publishing Group, Inc.
29 East 21st Street, New York, NY 10010

Photo Credits and Photo Illustrations: p. 4 by Maria Moreno; pp. 7, 20 by John Novajosky; pp. 8, 11, 16 by Seth Dinnerman; p. 12 © UPI/Corbis-Bettmann; p. 15 © David Brauchli/AP Photo; p. 19 Kelly Hahn.

First Edition

Layout and design: Erin McKenna

Middleton, Don.
    Dealing with discrimination / by Don Middleton.
            p.   cm. — (The conflict resolution library)
    Includes index.
    Summary: Discusses discrimination on both the general and individual levels and provides advice on dealing with and ending it.
    ISBN 0-8239-5270-3
    1. Discrimination—Juvenile literature. 2. Prejudices—Juvenile literature. 3. Toleration—Juvenile literature.
[1. Discrimination. 2. Prejudices.]   I. Title. II. Series.
    HM276.M495 1998
    305—dc21   98-11549
                                                                                          CIP
                                                                                          AC

Manufactured in the United States of America

Contents

1   What Is Discrimination?   5

2   Hating for No Reason   6

3   It Hurts Everyone   9

4   How Discrimination Starts   10

5   Your Rights   13

6   What You Look Like,
      What You Believe   14

7   The New Kid in Town   17

8   Not-So-Equal Rights   18

9   Different, but the Same   21

10   Breaking Down Walls   22

     Glossary   23

     Index   24

What Is Discrimination?

Discrimination (dis-KRIH-muh-NAY-shun) is an important word to know and understand. Discrimination means treating someone badly just because he or she is different from you. Whenever people are treated badly just for being who they are, it is wrong!

Sometimes only a person's feelings get hurt. But often the effects of discrimination are much worse. Kids get teased, left out of games, bullied, and even badly hurt. But what can be done about discrimination?

◄ *Discrimination can separate us from other people.*

Hating for No Reason

You meet kids all the time. Some you get to know better and they become your friends. Others don't always become friends. Usually they have different likes and dislikes. Even if they're not your friends, you still get along. But some people think they are better than others. They may believe that all people from a different group than their own are lazy or mean. This hating of others for no good reason is called **prejudice** (PREH-juh-dis). Prejudiced people often discriminate against others.

It's wrong to decide you don't like somebody without getting to know her. ▶

It Hurts Everyone

Unfortunately, the more different from others a person looks, speaks, or acts, the more likely it is that he or she will be treated unfairly. Today, **citizens** (SIH-tih-zens) who are new to the United States are still sometimes treated unfairly. Other groups, such as African Americans, Asians, and Latinos, often face prejudice, too. And some people discriminate against women, old or young people, or people who are sick.

◀ *If you decide you don't like someone because of how she looks, you might be missing out on making a good friend.*

How Discrimination Starts

Scott was part of the Hilltop Club. The kids in the club hung out together during lunch and after school every day. Other kids wanted to join them. But the club wouldn't be the same if the Hilltops let that happen. They had special rules! If you were a girl or a sissy, you couldn't be in the club. And all the Hilltops had to dress alike and have the same skin color. Some club members teased and bullied other students at school. Scott knew this was wrong and felt **guilty** (GIL-tee). When he quit the club, he knew it was the right thing to do.

Clubs that don't let people join because of how they look or what they believe are practicing discrimination. ▶

Your Rights

Most countries have laws that give each person **rights** (RYTS). Living, going to school, traveling, and working where we want to are some of those rights. Whenever someone tries to stop us from using any of our individual rights, they are discriminating against us, or **violating** (VY-uh-lay-ting) our rights. This can put us in an unfair or even a risky situation.

Sadly, in some countries, people don't even have basic rights. It can be very scary to live in these places.

◄ *In the 1950s and 1960s, Martin Luther King, Jr., fought for the rights of African Americans.*

What You Look Like, What You Believe

For thousands of years, people have faced discrimination because their skin is a different color, they practice a different religion, or just because they were born in a different country. When one group of people discriminates against another group, they sometimes do terrible things, such as hurting or killing others.

Even today, throughout the world, people openly show hatred for other people that they don't even know. This is wrong.

Discrimination can hurt everyone. It has made the children of Bosnia witnesses to war and violence. ▶

The New Kid in Town

Marcos was nervous when he and his family moved to a new neighborhood. He didn't see many kids around. Those that he did see playing on the sidewalk didn't look like they would want to be friends with him. One day, Marcos passed one of the kids on the street. "Hey!" the stranger shouted to Marcos. Oh, no, Marcos thought, he's going to pick a fight with me. Marcos kept walking. "Hey," the kid called again, "do you want to shoot some hoops?" "Sure," Marcos answered, glad that he was wrong about the stranger.

◄ *Even though kids may look different from you on the outside, you are probably a lot alike. That's what counts.*

Not-So-Equal Rights

Women have been treated differently from men throughout history. For a long time, women could not vote or own a house, a car, or any other property. Many women lost their jobs if they had a baby.

Today women have more **opportunities** (ah-per-TOO-nih-teez) and rights, but they still face discrimination. Often women can't get certain jobs because men think they can't do them. If they do get these jobs, they may be paid less than the men who are doing the same work.

There are many people who wrongly believe that women can't do certain jobs as well as men. ▶

Different, but the Same

Sean was invited to his friend Rosa's birthday party. He was excited even though he didn't know many of the kids that were going to be there. But as Sean's mother pulled up to Rosa's house, Sean changed his mind. All the kids going inside looked a lot different than he did. "I don't want to go," Sean told his mother. "Sean, just because some kids look different doesn't mean they're not like you on the inside." His mom was right. The kids at the party liked the same games as he did. Sean was glad he went.

◀ *The world would be a boring place if everyone were exactly alike.*

Breaking Down Walls

As we grow, we learn more and more about the world. We learn to trust the people we see every day. This includes our parents, friends, and teachers. They may look, talk, and think about things just as we do.

Some people wrongly believe that the way they are is the way all people should be. Part of growing up is learning that our world is full of nice people who look, talk, and even think differently than we do. This is what makes the world so interesting.

Glossary

citizen (SIH-tih-zen) A person who is born in or has the legal right to live in a certain country.

discrimination (dis-KRIH-muh-NAY-shun) The act of treating a person badly or unfairly just because he or she is different.

guilty (GIL-tee) When a person has done something wrong.

opportunity (ah-per-TOO-nih-tee) A good chance.

prejudice (PREH-juh-dis) Hatred of a group of people just for being different from you.

right (RYT) Something that everyone should be able to have or do.

violate (VY-uh-layt) To do something that breaks a law or a rule.

Index

A
African Americans, 9, 13
Asians, 9

B
bullying, 5, 10

C
citizens, 9
clubs, 10

F
friends, 6, 17, 21, 22

G
guilty, 10

H
hurting, 5, 14

J
jobs, 18

L
Latinos, 9
laws, 13

O
opportunities, 18

P
parents, 22
prejudice, 6, 9, 14
property, 18

R
religion, 14

rights, 13
  violating, 13
  voting, 18

S
school, 10, 13
skin color, 10, 14

T
teachers, 22
trust, 22

U
unfairness, 9

W
women, 9, 18
work, 13, 18

24